Primordial Strength System™
Basic Explosive Athletic Power

By Steven Helmicki

Copyright 2007 Steven Helmicki

ISBN 978-0-6151-4328-6

The Primordial Strength System™

Basic Explosive Athletic Power

www.PrimordialStrengthSystems.com

_____   _____

Trainees Name   Start Date

This book is dedicated to:

Fred Gellotte who appeared from nowhere to coach me to a national title, **elite** status and two Amateur **World Records**, my first top twenty-two ranking and my first number **seventeen USA squat**. He returned almost a decade later to encourage me to push through and win a sub-master **World Title** and a number twenty- two USA Squat.

Ken Leistner, Ralph Raiola, Mark Carthy, John Bott, Joey Almodovar, **Iron Island Gym**: All of you World Class and the most welcoming crew I have ever met.

Mr. Louie Simmons who has not received anywhere near the credit he deserves for the greatest advances in strength training in the last thirty years. Advancements in equipment have overshadowed the brilliance of his innovation.

To **West Side Barbell:** Only now do I realize the privilege it was to visit and get to train with the A Group in the mid to late 90's.

Mohan Ramanchandran: Esteemed professor of mathematics and adviser.

Randy Strossen and Elizabeth Hammond: Proud to be a part of **MILO..**

The Village Glenn Crew: Mr. Thomas Haney for being receptive to our lunacy. All the **lifting stars** that we produced, those were the days.

Nick Gampietro and East Aurora High School Football: The original experiments: R. Chen, twins C. and E. Giacomini, M.Gampietro.

Matt Roth: the epitome of working hard enough to live your dream. **Welcome to the Pro's.**

Demeris Johnson retired **NFL** wide-receiver with the **Miami Dolphins** and **Buffalo Bills** and owner of Perfecting Your Performance Inc.

Mike Wlosinski for creating an environment that provided world class equipment and developed world class lifters.

To Don Reinhoudt, Powerlifting god and **World's Strongest** man for supporting our early powerlifting meets and signing autographs for everyone. A truer gentleman there never was.

To Sgt. Bryce Rogers: **US Marine Corps** and soon to be the strongest Marine.

To **Jimmy** and **Tony Formato** the best football coaches ever.

To John Schweikhard and Chris Brysinski for backyard training sessions and filet on the grill. Also, thanks for keeping the **Buffalo Weightlifting Hall of Fame** alive.

To **Brooke Fineis** top female powerlifter and former training partner.

To **Julia Kauffman** top female powerlifter and former training partner.

Rob Nosek the human equivalent of rebar.

To **Brad Meyers** are first Frankenstein and scholarship from the VGC.

To **Cheryl Chambers**: Transplant **Olympic Gold** and Silver Medalist in the 100 and 200 hundred meters.

To all the **under dogs** and undersized athletes: Enter the coming pages and leave the manual an enthusiastic game changer.

The exhaustive list is to illustrate being **above the pettiness** that sometimes consumes iron sports. Thank you to anyone I may have overlooked. And that is that.

Covers designed by **Richard Walters Jr**. (aka Koolaid) at monker productions. He can be reached at RWaltersjr@hotmail.com.

Look around you at this exact moment in your training and be thankful for the time you have and the opportunity to train. It is truly a privilege. Be above any pettiness and avoid negativity.

Be a positive influence.

The call to Ray Chen: When football is over I will pass the powerlifting belt to you and challenge you to carry on the saga.

What they say about the training:

"Steve is the best I've seen as far as developing explosive power. He's got a proven system. In my opinion it is the best in the country."

Demeris Johnson

President of Perfecting Your Performance Inc./**NFL Alumni**

"Steve's system tripled my strength in 5 months and made advances in my explosive power that I can't believe. Now I realize I am only scraping the surface. In my **CFL** tryout I was placed against a big three year starting defensive tackle from the **University of Virginia** and me being from Division III St. John Fisher I was intimidated. I quickly realized the advantage of training the **Primordial Strength** Way when I dominated in one on ones. With hard work this system is the best for athletic explosive power. Now that I have my contract, I use Steve to prepare to start and will use him in the off season. I went from not starting in high school to being one of the top CFL tackles coming out of the US. Now I am a tackle with tight end explosive power and the ten and twenty times to prove it."

Matt Roth

St. Francis High School, St. John Fisher, **BC Lions** of the **CFL**

"This is some impressive stuff. I've never seen anything like it."

Jim Wendler

Former University of Arizona fullback and University of Kentucky Strength Coach/Senior Editor of Elite Fitness Systems/ West Side Graduate

Steven Helmicki was a Submaster **World** and National **Powerlifting Champion** in the 220lb class and an Amateur Open **National Champion** in the 198lb class. He has held two submaster **World Records** and two Amateur **Open World Records**. Mr. Helmicki had lifts ranked in **the top twenty in Powerlifting USA** from 1995-2003. He has also totaled **Elite**, holds national referee cards in the USPF, APF, AAU and served as the NY State Chairman for the USPF.

Mr. Helmicki has contributed to **_MILO_** (the benchmark in international strength publications) since 2000 and Elite Fitness Systems since 2007. A Certified USA Weightlifting Coach, Steven has apprenticed under every system that he could for the last twenty years progressing from basic bodybuilding, Nautilus, Mentzer approach to barbells, progressive overload powerlifting, West Side Barbell Powerlifting, strongman to the present **Primordial Strength System**™, which was incubated in the private **Metal Hardcore Garage Gym** under the watchful eye of a Neapolitan Mastiff named Maximus. The same Maximus made famous by his starring role in the Ironmind Catalog advertising the Headstrap for Hercules™.

Steven Helmicki has spent the last twenty years evolving a system that has produced incomparable explosive power on the athletic field. From Little Loop to the Professional Level, Mr. Helmicki has advanced the game of each trainee from **silver** and **gold medal** 100 and 200 meter transplant Olympians, professional hockey players, professional football players and youth lacrosse, baseball and football players. This system is applicable to all sports that require significant explosive power. **Primordial Strength System**™ is defined as a primary and **fundamental advancement of explosive power** through a **yearly system**. It maximizes leverages and eliminates weaknesses. The **Basic** Explosive Power Program is the first of four yearly phases: **Intermediate** Athletic Explosive Power; **Advanced** Athletic Explosive Power; **Professional** Athletic Explosive Power follow in the preceding years. **Primordial Strength Systems**™ covers the career span of athletic competition with unmatched explosive power.

The basic explosive power manual covers the initial youth introduction to sports training, the hypertrophy phase and finally the beginning of explosive power training. The in season training is the culmination of the first yearly cycle of the **Primordial Strength System™**.

The mentioning of brand names of specific equipment is intended to demonstrate that the tools for training are very important. **Primordial Strength Systems™** seeks the best and uses the best. Substitutions of other exercises and equipment may not produce the same results. Brand names are mentioned solely for the purpose of identifying what **Primordial Strength Systems™** uses in daily training practices.

As with any strength training program, professional guidance is always recommended. **Primordial Strength Systems™** recommends at the very least those coaches prescribing this program attend one of our seminars or have **Primordial Strength Systems™** do an on-site training seminar. **Primordial Strength Systems™** is also available for gym design and equipment selection. We only use the best and we recommend you do also.

For athletes utilizing this program in absence of professional guidance, the manual format assumes a working knowledge base of both old and newer movements. There are excellent data bases such as elitefitnesssystems.com which have exercise indexes.

The first question asked by a strength coach or the trainee themselves should be is their any injury, ache, pain or other reason the training session could be compromised. Adjustments to volume and tempo must be made according to the individual. A coach's greatest responsibility is to push the athlete to learn his own body by feel. This single skill will allow the continuous feedback necessary for the coach to prescribe individually within the framework of any system. Communication ultimately leads to success.

This system has led to more people jumping onto a 42" box, many with weight (and some high school freshman) than could be reasonably listed. The Skyscraper Club™ will be expanding and maybe it is your name that is next to go up.

Forthcoming titles:

The Primordial Strength Systems™ Intermediate Explosive Power manual

The Primordial Strength Systems™ Advanced Explosive Power Manual

The Primordial Strength Systems™ Professional Explosive Power Manual

The Art of the Neck and Traps

Primordial Strength Systems™ recommends using a testing site with Keiser Air equipment and safe field space with competent testing professionals. In WNY we recommend using Perfect Your Performance Incorporated in Sahlen Sports Park.

Our preferred vendor list:

Ironmind Enterprises

Elite Fitness Systems

Westside Barbell

Sorinex

Jump Stretch

Atomic Athletic

"Many arguments take place regarding the efficacy of certain training modalities. It seems everyone can tell you how to train, but few can show you. Primordial Strength Systems™ avoids the semantics and shows one how to be a devastating athlete. You become a doer not a talker. Someone other athletes whisper about in envy."-SCH

Take your team from 2-6 to 6-2 the following two seasons like East Aurora, New York High School did after employing this system.

Make it to the CFL from Division III like Matt Roth. Jump onto the forty-two inch box with a weight vest and fifteen pound dumbbells as a high school sophomore like Ray Chen. Throw the baseball eighty plus miles an hour as a high school freshman like Mark Gampietro. Add five inches to your vertical in five weeks like All-Western New York Football and All Star Basketball Player David Barnett. Not household names you say. That is exactly why you need to read further. We kept the blue chips out so you can't discount the system. We change the way games are played and turn average into frightening.

Train to Win. Period.™

Policy on Performance Enhancement

Our Philosophical and company policy states The Primordial Strength System™ espouses drug free training and all success stories cited are those achieved free of performance enhancement to the limit that Primordial Strength Systems™ can determine.

We urge each trainee to avoid the pitfalls of performance enhancement and seek the advice of a registered dietician to achieve maximum explosive power output through optimal natural food choices. Part of the testing protocols require the BIA which will measure your basal metabolic rate and allow you to plan to consume the necessary amount and quality of food to recover and grow.

Although we utilize a high volume system, we achieve restoration through active and natural means. Massage, chiropractic, physical therapy, acupuncture, flush workouts and high calorie, nutrient dense diets.

Athletes should train enhancement free.

No representative of Primordial Strength Systems™ shall discuss, direct or aid an athlete in the use of any performance enhancement agents.

Focus on hard work. You can feed all the oats you want to an ass, you won't get a racehorse!!!

The activities associated in this book with explosive athletic training are to be undertaken at the trainees own risk. When using these programs it is recommended that you be an experienced trainee whose joints and entire body are in excellent health, but this is not warranted to avoid injury. An injury sustained during the course of these programs is solely the responsibility of the user.

It is advisable to consult a physician prior to beginning any exercise program. A complete X-ray and CT scan should be undertaken prior to commencing serious neck training that is prescribed in some parts of the basic explosive power system.

When utilizing bands for training it is recommended that the entire stock of bands be inspected daily for tears and excessive wear and documented by staff in writing and kept for the life of the bands. Additionally, prior to each use, the trainer or trainee should inspect the bands. Even these precautionary measures cannot guarantee bands against breaking during the performance of the movements prescribe in Primordial Strength Systems™ Basic Athletic Explosive Power.

This manual is devoid of photographs because of their lack of ability to teach form to the degree we feel necessary. Do not attempt movements you are uncomfortable with or unfamiliar with. Consult with a strength coaching professional when questions or doubts arise. The corresponding DVD serves as the visual necessary for those who are unfamiliar with the movements prescribed.

Any call for a maximum attempt is defined by any lift performed without form break. If a lifter breaks form and gets the prior lift, we recommend stopping the lifter from further attempts. Safety should never be compromised in the performance of the lift. An athlete cannot continue to transform without mastering the preceding phases. Expect and demand form perfection. Always proceed methodically.

Introduction to the SWOT analysis as a tool for assessing strength, power, athletic skill or any aspect of planning for the athlete:

Strength	Weakness	Opportunity	Threat
Trainee is willing to squat with high intensity effort.	Trainee squats over knees, fails to sit back and stay Arched, doesn't explode from the feet.	clean squat form up to maximize power and minimize injury.	trainee does not adequately adapt To squat mechanics Inhibits explosive power development; becomes injured; premature athletic mortality.

This format can be used in the planning notes located in the back of this manual by both individual athletes and coaches. It is a tool Primordial Strength Systems™ has found to be an invaluable resource.

Primordial Strength Inc. in keeping with its philosophy of giving back to the community will donate a portion of the proceeds to assist those **NFL retirees** who are in need. It gives an opportunity to re-connect those beginning their athletic careers with those who have paved the road before us.

This level of brotherhood is an expectation of how all trainees, regardless of level should conduct themselves. The evolution of a system that brings out the best in each and every athlete, not only from the explosive power standpoint, but from the responsibility to bring those behind to their goals and support those who have served before us as an example of excellence.

Always give back to the sport.

The testing phase

Power production measurement on the Keiser Air Squat Machine/Tendo unit

Standing broad jump

Triple jump

Vertical jump

10 yard dash time

Measure for Snatch Grip-

Measure for Clean Grip-

Mark PVC with Snatch Grip tag

Mark PVC with Clean Grip tag

Height/Bodyweight

Bioelectrical Impedance Analysis- Record **B**asal **M**etabolic **R**ate; Hydration status; Fat Mass

Record on page 44

Initial Notes:

Introduction: This phase should be thoroughly established prior to commencing programming. If the trainee is embarking without professional coaching, he/she should create a plan of action in the back pages of this manual that will serve as the beginning of individual record keeping and goal establishment.

Emphasis of Form/Patience- At any point in form break the athlete and coach must maintain a willingness to step back and lower resistance if form breaks down. We try to teach position in lifts with the same intensity as position on the field.

Safety Statement: When a trainee gets hurt in the gym, they get hurt forever, sometimes physically, but always psychologically. Training is a privilege. Training is dangerous when it lacks focus.

The Role of the Coach: To push forward and pull back in a successful and supportive way that constantly has the athlete chomping at the bit of intensity, dying for the competition of what they love, ready to do battle for you with just a communication of body language.

The attitude for success: Critical encouragement is paramount to success, but continuous negative feedback is the key to disaster. Plan for success and re-plan for success and contingency plan. Always focus on the upside of all training dilemmas and never give up.

Mutual Support and Positive Environment: Do not train with anyone who cannot help you become a better athlete, either by them working so hard to catch up they push you or being so far ahead they push you to further your own expectations.

Setting Goals: Set them daily, weekly, yearly and for the training lifespan. Never become complacent.

Phase 1 work capacity development/explosive power introduction

This phase is intended as an introductory phase from high school athletes through the professionals, but it is also an excellent year round training formula for very young athletes that are on the verge of regular resistance training.

Day 1 This can be done in individual or class formats.

Jump Rope 10 minutes

10 standing broad jumps 30 seconds rest

PVC Bar Power Snatches 10 sets x 3 reps as rapid rest periods as ability allows

PVC Bar Snatch Grip Overhead Squats 3 sets x 10 reps 45 seconds rest

PVC Bar Push Jerks 10 sets x 3reps as rapid rest period as ability allows

Chins 2 sets x max reps 45 seconds rest

Medicine ball core swings 3 sets x 5 reps 45 seconds rest

Post Workout stretching up to 10 minutes in duration.

Day 2 This can be done in individual or class formats.

Jump Rope 10 minutes

Low Box jumps 10 sets x 2 reps every 30 seconds

PVC Bar Power Clean and Jerk 10 sets x 3 reps as rapid rest periods as ability allows

PVC Bar Jump Shrugs 10 sets x 3 reps as rapid rest period as ability allows

PVC Bar Front Squats 2 sets x 15 reps 30 seconds rest

Ceiling Rope Climb for time

Medicine ball throws sit-up/standing 3 sets x 5 reps 45 seconds rest

Post Workout stretching up to 10 minutes in duration.

Phase Two: Is 18 weeks of three six week sequences that begin with hypertrophy and advance to speed/explosive power introduction.

Warm-up: Jump rope 10 minutes

Bent arm pullovers x 25 reps x 1 set

Straight arm pullovers x 25 reps x 1 set

Remains the same until otherwise noted.

Completed prior to every workout.

First 6 weeks

Day 1

Manta Ray High Bar Close Stance Box squats 5 sets x 5 reps 1.5 minutes rest

Barbell Power Cleans 5 sets x 5 reps 1 minute rest

Close Grip Incline Presses 5 sets x 5 reps 2 minutes rest

Trap Bar Deadlifts 1 set x 20 reps

Core dumbbell/kettlebell swings 3 sets x 6 reps 45 seconds rest

Neck Harness (recommend Ironmind Headstrap Fit For Hercules)
5 sets front/5 sets back x 12 reps 1 minute rest

Post Workout stretch only the tight/stressed areas 10 minutes maximum.

Day 2

Low Bar Wide Stance Box Squat 10 sets x 2 reps 45 seconds rest

Snatch Grip High Pulls 5 sets x 5 reps 1.5 minutes rest

Dumbbell Overhead Press 5 sets x 5 reps 2 minutes rest

Dumbbell Power Cleans 3 sets x 8 reps 2 minutes rest

Dumbbell Hammer Curls 5 sets x 5 reps 1 minute rest

Neck Harness 5 sets front/5 sets back x 20 reps x 1 minute rest

Post Workout stretch only the tight/stressed areas 10 minute maximum.

Second 6 weeks

Day 1

Manta Ray High Bar Close Stance Box Squats

8 sets x 3 reps 45 seconds rest

Barbell Power Cleans

10 sets x 2 reps 1.5 minutes rest

Landmine One Arm Press

5 sets x 3 reps explosively

Hungarian Core Blaster Swings

6 sets x 5 reps 45 seconds rest

Box Jumps-jump onto three successive boxes 3 reps to 70% of max height

Neck Harness 2 sets front/ 2 sets back x 30 reps 1 minute rest

(Recommend Ironmind's a Headstrap fit for Hercules)

Day 2

Trap Bar Deadlift 5 sets x 3 reps 1 minute rest

Power Snatches 5 sets x 2 reps 2 minutes rest

Close Grip Inclines 3 sets x 5 reps 1.5 minutes rest

Landmine twists 3 sets x 8 reps 45 seconds rest

High Bar squats 40% of day 1 poundage x 1 set x 10 reps

Day 3

Wide Stance Low Bar Power Box Squats 12 sets x 2 reps 35 seconds rest

Power Clean and Jerks 5 sets x 2 reps 2 minute rest

Empty Bar Overhead Squats 2 sets x 15 reps 1.5 minutes rest

Band sprints; attach Jump stretch bands to the back of the lifting belt

2 average bands 5 sets x 3 starts with 30 seconds rest

Neck Harness 2 sets front/2 sets back x 30 reps 1.5 minutes rest

Third Six Weeks

Day 1

Manta Ray High Bar Squats 5 sets x 3 reps 45 seconds rest

Standing Manta Ray Calf Raises 2 sets x 15 reps 1 minute rest

Power Clean and Strict Press 3 sets x 2 reps 1 minute rest

Close grip inclines 5 sets x 3 reps

Jump stretch two light bands attached to belt sprints 7 sets x 3 reps 15 seconds rest between starts

Day 2

Wide Stance Low Bar Power Squats 8 sets x 3 reps 30 seconds rest

Seated calf Raises 2 sets x 15 reps 1 minute rest

Snatch Grip High Pulls 10 sets x 2 reps 30 seconds rest

Dumbbell Incline Press 7 sets x 3 reps 50 seconds rest

Neck harness 7 sets x 10 reps front/back 1 minute rest

Flush workout-Completed after Phase 2 and prior to Phase 3.

3 exercises of trainees choice 125 reps on each movement in 5 minutes or less for each movement.

Phase Three: Three-Five weeks in duration.

Day 1

One leg MVP push-offs-alternative one legged alternating explosive leg press

5 reps x 6sets 30 seconds rest

MVP Explosive jumps-alternate exercise standing dumbbell vertical jumps
8 reps x 6 sets 30 seconds rest

Keiser air squats 10 sets x 3reps full speed-alternative medium stance bar squat
30 seconds rest
35% x 3 sets
40% x 3 sets
45% x 4 sets
1 set 20 reps super slow 50%

Landmine Press 3 reps x 6 sets 45 seconds rest

Snatch Grip High Pulls
10 reps x 6 sets 1 minute rest

Upright rows
2 sets x 10 reps 1 minute rest

Incline close-grip presses
3 reps x 6 sets
30 seconds rest

Landmine twists
4 sets x 8 reps 1 minute rest

Dumbbell/kettlebell swings
20 reps x 2 sets

Chins maximum additional weight

2 sets x 8-12 reps

Chin Position Hang for time

Ironmind guide gripper 1 set x max reps

Day 2

Low box jumps 40lb, 50lb, 60lb x 5 reps plus vest no more than 50 seconds rest

Keiser power rack squat-alternative power rack band pin squat 185-200lbs band tension

Empty bar band weight max

Maximum Air tension plus 55lbs bar x 1 max effort

Keiser Front press-alternative light band pin front press maximum

55lb bar weight plus maximum air tension x 1 max effort

Reverse grip bent rows

13 sets x 5 reps   (end with maximum reps @65lbs x 45reps is high range)

Land mine trap flexed high pulls

13 sets x 3 reps 30 seconds rest

Dumbbell/kettlebell swings

3 sets x 35 reps 1 minute rest

Neck helmet bridges on Bosu Trainer 1 x 15 front and back

Day 3

Explosive squats on Keiser Air Squat Machine-alternative wide stance box squats 45% x 3 sets; 50% x 3 sets; 55% x 3 sets; 60% x 3 sets

12 sets x 4 reps 30 seconds rest

Sled drags 6 front/ 6 back 4 plates; 2 plates; 1 plate
6 sets x 25 yards 45 seconds rest

Band starts attached to belt
2 sets x 3-5 reps light band; two light bands 2 sets 3-5 reps 30 seconds rest

Dumbbell Cleans and Presses
2 reps x 20lbs; 30lbs; 40lbs x 4 rotations non-stop

Decline sit-ups
4 sets x 5 reps

Landmine Devastation
Combat grip x 8 reps per side immediately followed by
Twists x 8 reps per side 3 sets x 45 seconds rest

Pinch grip plate curls maximum weight to achieve rep range
5 sets x 8 reps 45 seconds rest

Flush Workout

5 lifts of the trainees or coaches choice; extremely light resistance 100 reps x 1 set each exercise.

Re-Test: Record results on page 51.

Phase Four: Three to five weeks in duration.

Day 1

Squat on Keiser-alternative High bar medium stance squat 40%
2 sets x 15 reps 1 minute rest

Landmine one arm power snatches
4 reps x 6 sets 45 seconds rest

Landmine on arm press
4 reps x 6 sets 45 seconds rest

Ironmind Eagle Loops chins
6 sets x 1 rep add weight

Spread eagle sit-ups
3 sets x 5 reps

Neck harness (Ironmind A Headstrap Fit For Hercules is recommended)
25 reps x 1 set front/back

Day 2

Speed squat on Keiser Air-alternative low bar wide stance squat
50%1 rep max x 12 sets x 4reps 30 seconds rest

Box jumps Low box vest plus 20's, 30's, 40's 2 sets x 3 reps with each pair 40 seconds rest

Dumbbell/kettlebell Swings 6 sets x 6 reps 30 seconds rest

Landmine Presses (Explode) 6 sets x 6 reps 30 seconds rest

Manta Ray Hise shrugs/Standing Calf Raise 3 sets x 10 reps 50 seconds rest

Ironmind Eagle Loops Chins 4 sets x 4 reps 1 minute rest

Ironmind Sport Gripper 1 set x max reps

Phase Five: 3-5 Weeks in duration.

Day 1
Warm-up
Jump rope 10 minutes

2 sets pullovers x 25 reps
Shoulder pre-hab

Yoke/Barbell Walk with Weight
Week one Bodyweight x 15 yards x 13 trips 1.5 minute rest

Week two bodyweight plus 10% x 20 yards x 9 trips
Week three bodyweight plus 15% x 10 yards x 11 trips
Week four 50% bodyweight x 50 yards x 2 trips

Stiff-legged deadlifts-maximum weight trainee can handle to achieve rep scheme
2 sets x 15 reps 1 minute rest

Kettlebell/ Dumbbell Swings

Heavyweight x 5 reps x 9 sets 45 seconds rest

Rest 3 minutes

Double kettlebell/dumbbell swings 50% heavy day x 10 reps x 7 sets 30 seconds rest

Rest 5 minutes

Landmine single arm rows
5 reps x 11 sets 45 seconds rest

Land mine single arm high pulls flexed trap
2 reps x 11 sets 45 seconds rest

Landmine single arm press
50% max x 20 sets x 2 reps speed 45 seconds rest

Ironmind Trainer gripper 1 set x max reps

Land mine one arm standing curls 5 sets x 3 reps 45 seconds

Ironmind Eagle Loop Barbell Curls x 5sets x 10 reps 45 seconds rest

Neck harness (Ironmind A Headstrap Fit for Hercules) 50 reps x 2 sets front and back 2 minutes rest

Day 2
Warm-up
Jump rope 10 minutes

Pullovers 3 sets x 25 reps

Shoulder pre-hab

Speed squat day

50% plus 100 lb band tension x 12 sets x 2 reps 45 seconds rest

55% plus 100 lb band tension 12sets x 2 reps 45 seconds rest

60% plus 100 lb band tension 10sets x 2 reps 45 seconds rest

65% plus 100 lb band tension 8 sets x 2 reps 45 seconds rest

Post speed work

Seated Goodmornings x 15 reps x 3 sets 1 minute rest

Manta-Ray Calf Raises 4 sets x 6 reps 45 seconds rest

Manta-Ray Hise Shrugs 4 sets x 15 reps 45 seconds rest

Incline Dumbbell Curls 11 sets x 3 reps (heavy) 15 seconds rest

Spread eagle sit-ups 5 sets x 3 reps 45 seconds rest

Day 3

Warm-up

Jump rope 10 minutes

Pullovers 3 sets x 25 reps

Shoulder pre-hab

Bench Day

Tempo 1 minute to 1.5 minutes rest, except on max 235/195 use 2 minutes-3 minutes rest.

Bench day 235 reps for combine/195 for younger athletes who will test 185lbs.

Warm-up bar x 8; 95 x 6; 135 x 3; 185 x 1; 235 x maximum reps (15)x 2 sets

Double mini-bands behind the back bench plus 135lb/95lbs bar weight for 1 set maximum reps

Close grip inclines 5 sets x 5 reps

Front plate raises 4 sets x 6 reps

Face Pulls 4 sets x 15 reps

Bent –over power rows 7 sets x 5 reps

Dumbbell hammer curls 4 sets x 3 reps

Land mine twists 5 sets x 3 reps

Neck Harness 4 sets x 20 reps

Week off

Re-Test: Record results on Page 56.

Phase 6

12 weeks

Warm-up: jump rope 10 minutes

Band hip adductor/abductor

Straight arm pullover

Bent arm pullover

Super mans

Day 1

21 vertical Verimax jumps 15 seconds rest/alternative 21 dumbbell vertical jumps

3 minutes rest/water

21 broad jumps 15 seconds rest

40% 1rm speed box squats

4 reps x 10 sets 45 seconds rest

Power rows
4 reps x 10 sets 45 seconds rest

Snatch grip high pulls
4 reps x 10 sets 45 seconds rest

Kettlebell/Dumbbell swings
10 sets x 5 reps 45 seconds rest

Day 2
Barbell Jump shrugs 5 sets x 2 reps 30 seconds rest

80% 5 sets x 2 reps pin squat 1.5 minutes rest

Hise shrugs 5 sets x 5 reps 1 minute rest

500 combined repetitions of abdominal work of athletes choosing; minimum of 12 movements.

Day 3

Weight walk bodyweight x 10 yards x 8 trips 45 seconds rest

Dumbbell power cleans and presses 5 sets x 2 reps heavy 45 seconds rest

Clean grip high pulls 5 sets x 2 reps heavy 45 seconds rest

Land mine rows 5 sets x 5 reps heavy 45 seconds rest

Phase Seven

Day 1

30 yards of broad jumps x 3 sets with 35 seconds rest

High pin squat 6-8inch movement
Max effort until miss

Standing calf raises heavy
3 sets x 5 reps

Seated calf raises heavy
3 sets x 5 reps

Land mine press
Heavy singles x 6 sets 45 seconds rest

Landmine rows
Heavy triples x 6 sets 45 seconds rest

Dumbbell swings
Pair of 40's
Pair of 30's
Pair of 20's
Pair of 15's
Max reps 1min between sets

Neck bridges on Bosu trainer
2 sets front/ 2 sets back max reps

Day 2

Incline pin press just off chest
Max effort until miss

Overhead dumbbell press
13 sets x 3 reps 45 seconds rest

Chins with weight vest
3 sets max reps 1 minute rest

Clean grip high pulls
7 sets x 2 reps 45 seconds rest

Barbell Manta Ray Hise shrugs
3 sets x 20 reps 1 minute rest

Face Pulls 3 grips x 25 reps each 45 seconds rest

Overhead Squats in the Power Rack
10 reps x 3 sets 1 minute rest

Land Mine Combat Grip
Twist –explode-twist
5 reps x 5 sets 35 seconds rest

Neck Bridges on Bosu trainer
3 sets front/3 sets back max reps

Dumbbell/Kettlebell Swings

4 sets x 6 reps 30 seconds rest

Day 3

Weight Walk yoke or barbell

Bodyweight x 20 yards x 8 trips 45 seconds rest

Keiser Air Speed Squats/ barbell squats

16 sets x 2 reps 30 seconds rest 65% of 1 rm

Barbell Jump Shrugs

8 sets x 4 reps 45 seconds rest

Barbell Snatch Grip Shrugs

5 sets x 4 reps 45 seconds rest

Barbell Snatch Grip Power Rows

5 sets x 4 reps 45 seconds rest

Dumbbell/kettlebell Standing Hammer Curls

15 sets x 3 reps heavy 25 seconds rest

Landmine Twists

12 sets x 4 reps 45 seconds rest

Decline Sit-Ups

6 sets x 6 reps heavy 45 seconds rest

Kettlebell/dumbbell Swings

2 sets x 20 reps 45 seconds rest

Kettlebell/dumbbell Swings

1 sets x 40 reps

Neck Bridges on Bosu trainer

2 sets front/2 sets back

Flush Workout

7 exercises of trainees/coaches choice for 50 reps x 1 set each exercise

Phase 8

Extreme Work Load Phase 2-5 weeks depending on burnout.

Day 1

Bodyweight Yoke/barbell walks 12 trips x 15 yards 30 seconds rest 10% over bodyweight

Dumbbell Power Cleans pair of 10lbs, 20lbs, 30lbs, 40lbs, 50lbs, 60lbs x 3 reps in succession

Bent over power rows 13 sets x 2 reps 30 seconds rest use resistance that does not allow bar speed to slow

Power Shrugs 13 sets x 3 reps 30 seconds rest

Vest weighted chins 4 sets x max reps 45 seconds rest

Landmine twists 6 sets x 5 reps

Decline sit-ups 3 sets x 5 reps max weight

Helmet neck bridges on Bosu trainer front/back 5 sets x 10 reps

Neck stretch

Day 2

Triple Jumps progressive weights pair 20lb, 30lb, 40lb dumbbells 4 sets of each weight with 45 seconds rest

Low Box squat 40% 1 rep max x 13 sets x 2 reps 45 seconds rest

Standing Calf Raises 7 sets x 7 reps 30 seconds rest

Seated Calf Raises 7 sets x 7 reps 30 seconds rest

Close grip incline max single

Hammer Curls 16 sets x 3 reps 30 seconds rest

Two arm core swings dumbbell/kettlebell 13 sets x 5 reps 30 seconds rest

Day 3

Low box jumps with 20 lb dumbbells x 12 sets x 2 reps 30 seconds rest

Pin Quarter Squat Maximum

30% 1 rep max speed deadlift 12 sets x 1 rep 15 seconds rest

Hise shrugs 25 reps x 2 sets

Landmine combat grip/Single Arm Dumbbell/ kettlebell swing

10 sets x 5 reps superset

Helmet Neck Bridges 3 sets x max reps

Stand on Ball for time

Stretch

Recuperation Day

20% 1 rep max squat x 50 reps x 1 set

10% 1 rep max dumbbell presses x 50 reps x 1 set

Light band pushdowns x 100 reps x 1 set

Dumbbell biceps curls x 50 reps x 1 set

Dumbbell/kettlebell swings x 50 reps x 1 set

Treadmill walk 20 minutes slow pace

Week off

Re-test: Record results on page 63.

Phase 9

Velocity Phase – This six week phase should occur anywhere from 7-9 weeks out from camp.

Day 1

Rotate 40%, 45%, 50% 1 rep max barbell speed parallel box squat with light band attached 15 sets x 2 reps 30 seconds rest.

2-4 minutes rest/water

Band starts: 5 sets x 2 double average bands 30 seconds rest

Band starts: 5 sets x 2 double light bands 30 seconds rest

2-4 minutes rest/water

Keiser Air Sprint Machine 4 sets x 17 strides at 100% Bodyweight 30 seconds rest or Sled sprints 50% bodyweight 40 yards 45 seconds rest

2-4 minutes rest/water

Manta Ray Hise Shrugs 100 reps in seven minutes

2-4 minutes rest

Straight Bar Biceps Curl 13 sets x 3 reps 35 seconds rest

Landmine Combat Grip 3 reps per side for time. 1 straight minute. Add 10 seconds per week.

Day 2

Rotate 35%, 40%, 45% 1 rep max barbell incline speed press with mini-bands attached 15 sets x 2 reps 30 seconds rest

2-4 minutes rest/water

Speed Power Rows 16 sets x 2 reps with 35% 1rep max 35 seconds rest

2-4 minutes rest/water

Land mine one arm presses 3 reps each hand rotating back and forth for 1 minute straight. Add 10 seconds each week.

2-4 minutes rest

Band Triceps Pushdowns 200 reps in seven minutes or less

2-4 minutes rest/water

Landmine Twists 13 sets x 3 reps 40 seconds rest

Captains of Crush Trainer or Number 1 for max reps x 2 sets

Day 3

Rotate 35%, 40%, 45% 1 rep max barbell speed deadlift with mini-bands attached to platform 15 singles on 20 seconds rest

2-4 minutes rest/water

Jumps over stationary bench for time: Back and forth for 1 minute straight. Add ten seconds per week.

6 minutes rest

Power Shrugs 13 sets x 4 reps 40 seconds rest

3 minutes rest

Reverse Straight Bar Curls 12 sets x 3 reps 30 seconds rest

Neck Harness 125 reps front/back in 7 minutes or less

Dumbbell/Kettlebell Swings 13 sets x 5 reps 40 seconds rest

Rest 3 minutes

Dumbbell/Kettlebell Swings 1 set x 75 reps

Re-Test: Record Results on Page 65.

Phase 10

In-Season Training: Up to two additional sets of each exercise can be performed if the athlete has the energy. As always, while injured or less than one-hundred percent it may be necessary to reduce volume or eliminate movements completely. Please consult professional sports medicine assistance prior to training on the **Primordial Strength System** if and when you have suffered an athletic injury.

Day 1

Yoke/Barbell Weight Walk

50% bodyweight x 6 trips of 15 yards 30 seconds rest

Speed squats 40% 1 rep max x 5 sets x 2 reps 20 seconds rest

Standing calf raises 2 sets x 12 reps 30 seconds rest

Seated calf raises 2 sets x 12 reps 30 seconds rest

Snatch grip shrugs 2 sets x 6 reps 30 seconds rest

Snatch grip power rows 2 sets x 6 reps 30 seconds rest

Hammer curls 4 sets x 5 reps 20 seconds rest

Kettlebell/dumbbell Swings 1 set x 25 reps

Neck bridges on Bosu trainer x 2 sets x 10 reps

Day 2

alternate lowest box jumps 15lb dumbbells x 4 sets x 2 reps 20 seconds rest/

triple jumps with 5lb dumbbells 4 sets 30 seconds rest/broad jumps with 10lb dumbbells 5 sets 30 seconds rest

Low pin squat 70% max x 2 sets x 3-5 reps depending on feel 1.5 minutes rest

Close grip incline 70% max x 2 sets x 3-5 reps depending on feel 1.5 minutes rest

Hise shrugs 2 sets x 20 reps 1 minute rest

Band triceps pushdown 50 reps in three minutes or less

Neck harness 2 sets x 25 reps 1 minute rest

Landmine 2 sets combat grip; two sets twists x 12 reps 45 seconds rest

Post Competition

After games take a default squat of 25% x 14 reps

15 minutes on the treadmill

Stretching Routine

Primordial Strength Systems™
Intermediate Athletic Explosive Power.

Initial Goal Setting:

Initial Testing Phase Results:

Power production measurement Keiser Air Squat Machine/Tendo unit: _____

Standing broad jump_____

Triple jump_____

Vertical jump_____

10 yard dash time_____

Measure for Snatch Grip_____

Measure for Clean Grip_____

Mark PVC with Snatch Grip tag_____

Mark PVC with Clean Grip tag_____

Height_____

Bodyweight_____

Bioelectrical Impedence Analysis:

Hydration Status:_____

BMR_____

Fat Mass_____

Phase Notes: A Page for each phase to reference any indicators that effect training. Mood, weights, recovery, new goals, etc. Can be filled in by coach or trainee. The more detailed this information is the greater the individualization of the programming takes place.

The details are critical.

Phase 1:

Phase 2:

Phase 3:

Re-Test

Power production measurement Keiser Air Squat Machine/Tendo unit:_____

Standing broad jump_____

Triple jump_____

Vertical jump_____

10 yard dash time_____

Height_____

Bodyweight_____

BIA Results:

Hydration status:_____

BMR_____

Fat Mass_____

Phase 4:

Phase 5:

Re-Test

Power production measurement Keiser Air Squat Machine/Tendo unit:_____

Standing broad jump_____

Triple jump_____

Vertical jump_____

10 Yard dash time_____

Height_____

Bodyweight_____

BIA results:

Hydration status:_____

BMR:_____

Fat Mass:_____

Phase 6:

Phase 7:

Phase 8:

Re-Test

Power production measurement Keiser Air Squat Machine/Tendo unit:_____

Standing broad jump_____

Triple jump_____

Vertical jump_____

10 Yard dash time_____

Height_____

Bodyweight_____

BIA Results:

Hydration Status:_____

BMR_____

Fat Mass_____

Phase 9:

Re-Test

Power production measurement Keiser Air Squat Machine/Tendo unit:_____

Standing broad jump_____

Triple jump_____

Vertical jump_____

10 Yard dash time_____

Height_____

Bodyweight_____

BIA Results:

Hydration status:_____

BMR_____

Fat Mass_____

Comparative Test: Review initial testing in comparison to final re-test.

Record improvements:

Phase 10:

Date Completed_____

Believe in yourself when no one else will. Soon everyone will believe in you even when you cannot. Your wherewithal is your success. Never concede to what stands in your way.

Thank God.

RIP #34 Shaun "Earl" Little
I never got to say Goodbye.
Peace.